POVERTY I DIVORCE YOU ABSOLUTELY

BAMIDELE BELLO

Library of Congress Control Number: 2015932604

ISBN-13: 978-0-692-38123-6
ISBN: 0692381236

www.kingdombuilderspublications.com
kbpublications@sc.rr.com

Poverty I Divorce You Absolutely

This Book Belongs to

DEDICATION

This book is dedicated to the Almighty God, the creator of the Heavens and Earth; who inspired me to believe in Him; who kept my faith strong even when the storms of life almost swallowed me. I also dedicate these writings to the family of Holy Mountain International Ministries (Blessed House) for their support and continued belief in Jesus Christ of Nazareth.

CONTENTS

ACKNOWLEDGEMENTS

This Book is dedicated to God Almighty who gives me opportunity to be alive to spread the word to many people. God has been so gracious to me in life that I cannot thank Him enough. Glory be to His Holy name.

I also want to thank my wife Rhonda for helping me in my Christian journey. Her talents, her patience, and her love for Jesus have been a great blessing.

This book would not be complete without mentioning all the efforts of my publisher Louise Smith from Kingdom Builders Publications. When I was struggling to pick a design for my book cover page, Mrs. Louise came with a wonderful cover page that I could not resist. She motivated me every day since my wife Rhonda connected me to her. May the God Almighty reward her continually in Jesus name.

Our God is a good God.

We serve a Big God.

Poverty I Divorce You Absolutely

⌒∞∞∞⌒

Chapter One

Poverty is a state or condition of having little or no money, goods, or means of support; condition of being poor.

One Philosophy of life is that "You will never become rich, until you hate poverty." When you stay too long in poverty your spirit, soul, and body will adjust to poverty, until you realize that God plans for your live is to live in abundant, you will not get out of poverty until you make up your mind and divorce poverty absolutely without contestant, you will not be able to meet up your financial obligations.

Financial obligations are a state of an responsibility to pay money to another party. The obligation may arise from borrowing funds or from a legal action, also known as liability. When you decide to live your entire life in poverty, a tendency may lead you to think that you will be confused, rejected, unwanted, and hated. Life will not be meaningful to you. The wind of life will start to carry you to different directions of failure and confusion. Insult will start to come from every direction including your children and siblings and other family members.

The thief cometh not, but for to steal, and to kill, and to destroy: I am come that they might have life, and that they might have it more abundantly. John 10:10 KJV

Poverty is a thief that comes to steal, rob, and to kill your joy in life. You need to put an end to poverty with immediate effect!

Beloved, I wish above all things that thou mayest prosper and be in health, even as thy soul prospereth. 3 John 2

Jesus has promised Christians health and wealth if they have the level of faith that produces. However, the New Testament usually emphasizes a radically different result of following Christ. We are told that we will be persecuted, that Christ's message is divisive; that we will need to take up our cross and follow Him; that the normative expectation for Christian is suffering. Job promotions, new cars, and throwing away crutches are not among the fringe benefits offered by Jesus Christ for Christians.

My brothers and Sisters in Christ, now is the right time for you to wake up and claim all the blessings that God has bestrew upon your life in the book of Deuteronomy 28:2-3.

2And all these blessings shall come on thee, and overtake thee, if thou shalt hearken unto the voice of the LORD thy God.
3Blessed shalt thou be in the city, and blessed shalt thou be in the field.

God has commanded us to be blessed in the city, and blessed in the field, but until we open our spiritual eyes and declare war against the stronghold blocking our destiny, prosperity will not come. The enemies of progress are part of the ones hindering our blessing, so you need a prosperity that will embarrass your enemies.

ꙮ PRAYER POINTS ꙮ

→ *Lord My God, I reject poverty absolutely in Jesus name, my*

→ *Daddy in Heaven, disconnect the source of poverty and make me rich in Jesus name.*

→ *Miracle at the zero moment, locate me and let me be on top in Jesus name.*

→ *Lord Jesus, visit the evil bank by fire, thunder and by hammer and release my money in captivity in Jesus name.*

Poverty Cycle

⚬ᴓᴓᴓᴓᴓ

Chapter Two

Believe it or not, poverty has a cycle. One generation in a family's heritage have to stand up and break that cycle of *poverty yoke* before other family members will start to enjoy the blessings God has commanded. This is where the prayer of faith and interceding comes in and fight every yoke of financial predicament in the family. Many Christians don't believe in the yoke of poverty in family, most especially in the western world. The system can be deceiving but I will tell you the truth, poverty is a spirit that you need to fight. If you are still going out working forty hours in a week, paying car note, struggle to pay your rent brothers and sister you need to pray so that God can deliver you from the spirit of poverty.

God has chosen you to be the right person to stand in the gap for your family. As you are reading this book, check your family heritage, ask yourself, how many millionaires do you have in your family? Are you one of the millionaires? If your answer is "No" then examine yourself and take poverty cycle serious, and pray for your family's deliverance from poverty. You are destined to be above not beneath.

For I know the thoughts that I think toward you, saith the LORD, thoughts of peace, and not of evil, to give you an expected end. Jeremiah 29:11 KJV

So shall my word be that goeth forth out of my mouth: it shall not return unto me void, but it shall accomplish that which I please, and it shall prosper in the thing whereto I sent it. Isaiah 55:11

The society in which we live, particularly the western world, have been hoodwinked thinking that they are making it because of the governmental trickery to be on a little unemployment voucher, but in actuality these voucher holders are blinded in their understanding. This is nothing more than the poor being enslaved to the destiny of poverty. It is time for us to wake up and do something to change our mentality of getting vouchers from government and become the lender; not the borrower. Here is a question for you. Does the money you received from the government enough for you to be blessed like the promises found in *Deuteronomy 28:2-13?*

The answer is a resounding absolutely, most emphatically NO!

CAUSES OF POVERTY

→ *Laziness or Moral Foolishness*

Laziness is disinclination to activity or exertion despite having the ability to do so.

Laziness is when opportunities are out there and one refuses to go and benefit from it.

The Bible made it clear. Paul writes,

For we hear that there are some which walk among you disorderly, working not at all, but are busybodies
2 Thessalonians 3:11

Many rely on taking wealth and properties that belongs to others i.e. (stealing, kleptomania, coveting).

Let him that stole steal no more: but rather let him labour, working with his hands the thing which is good, that he may have to give to him that needeth. Ephesians 4:28

The prodigal son returned to his father and was received with great joy. It is never too late for lazy people to return to Jesus and then look for something to do that will prosper their life. No time is a waste when it comes to Jesus.

[11]And he said, A certain man had two sons:
[12]And the younger of them said to [his] father, Father,
give me the portion of goods that falleth [to me]. And he
divided unto them [his] living.
[13]And not many days after the younger son gathered all
together, and took his journey into a far country, and there
wasted his substance with riotous living.
[14]And when he had spent all, there arose a mighty famine
in that land; and he began to be in want.
[15]And he went and joined himself to a citizen of that
country; and he sent him into his fields to feed swine.
[16]And he would fain have filled his belly with the husks
that the swine did eat: and no man gave unto him.
[17]And when he came to himself, he said, How many hired
servants of my fathers have bread enough and to spare, and
I perish with hunger!
[18]I will arise and go to my father, and will say unto him,
Father, I have sinned against heaven, and before thee,
[19]And am no more worthy to be called thy son: make me
as one of thy hired servants.
[20]And he arose, and came to his father. But when he was
yet a great way off, his father saw him, and had
compassion, and ran, and fell on his neck, and kissed him.
[21]And the son said unto him, Father, I have sinned
against heaven, and in thy sight, and am no more worthy
to be called thy son.
[22]But the father said to his servants, Bring forth the best

robe, and put [it] on him; and put a ring on his hand, and
shoes on [his] feet:
23 And bring hither the fatted calf, and kill [it]; and let us
eat, and be merry:
24 For this my son was dead, and is alive again; he was
lost, and is found. And they began to be merry.
Luke 15:11-24

11 And that ye study to be quiet, and to do your own
business, and to work with your own hands, as we
commanded you;
12 That ye may walk honestly toward them that are
without, and [that] ye may have lack of nothing.
1 Thessalonians 4:11-12.

Hard work with persistent prayer gets God's attention on your behalf for favor and blessings.

→ Sudden Disasters that Destroyed wealth, or calamities

Sudden disaster such as droughts that inhibited farmers from creating wealth can cause poverty. Successful farming requires modern day machinery and good markets. Limited technology and markets made recovery from loss much more difficult in the first century, and this contributed to ongoing poverty.

*4What man of you, having an hundred sheep, if he lose one
of them, doth not leave the ninety and nine in the
wilderness, and go after that which is lost, until he find it?
5And when he hath found [it], he layeth [it] on his
shoulders, rejoicing.
6And when he cometh home, he calleth together [his]
friends and neighbours, saying unto them, Rejoice with me;
for I have found my sheep which was lost.
7I say unto you, that likewise joy shall be in heaven over
one sinner that repenteth, more than over ninety and nine
just persons, which need no repentance.
8Either what woman having ten pieces of silver, if she lose
one piece, doth not light a candle, and sweep the house, and
seek diligently till she find [it]?
9And when she hath found [it], she calleth [her] friends
and [her] neighbours together, saying, Rejoice with me; for
I have found the piece which I had lost."
Luke 15: 4- 9*

→ Oppressing the Poor

God gives you wealth to be a blessing to others; not to oppress others. God does not allow covetousness. The idea of coveting what doesn't belong to you can bring you into poverty.

15 And he said unto them, Take heed, and beware of covetousness: for a man's life consisteth not in the abundance of the things which he possesseth.
16 And he spake a parable unto them, saying, The ground of a certain rich man brought forth plentifully:
17 And he thought within himself, saying, What shall I do, because I have no room where to bestow my fruits?
18 And he said, This will I do: I will pull down my barns, and build greater; and there will I bestow all my fruits and my goods.
19 And I will say to my soul, Soul, thou hast much goods laid up for many years; take thine ease, eat, drink, [and] be merry.
20 But God said unto him, [Thou] fool, this night thy soul shall be required of thee: then whose shall those things be, which thou hast provided?
21 So [is] he that layeth up treasure for himself, and is not rich toward God."
Luke 12 :17-21

In the olden days, creating wealth was difficult

because the vast majority of the population were employed in subsistence farming. Riches were commonly accumulated through oppressing workers, exploiting slaves, and taxing people heavily which most commonly added to the worker's problem.

→ Problems associated with living in a fallen world

The underdeveloped society face numerous challenges in the areas of old age, illness, or loss of family members. Poverty ratio in underdeveloped countries need God's intervention because people are not exposed to things that will take them out of poverty. Moreover, some are not exposed to the teachings of the Bible enough to see become enlightened. Widows and children in these areas of the world are not benefiting in any areas according to Bible.

3Honour widows that are widows indeed.
4But if any widow have children or nephews, let them learn first to shew piety at home, and to requite their parents: for that is good and acceptable before God. 1 Timothy 5:3-4.

Many Christians live in poverty because of the ignorance of poverty in their lives. I have had many discussions with some who say, "This is

America; we don't have the spirit of poverty, we are wealthy. We are blessed." My question is, are we are wealthy? Are we blessed? We do not have poverty in America? There is still homelessness in every city in America; people hanging around the street begging for change and shelters are over populated.

Christians need to wake up; poverty eradication is a challenge responsibility for every Christian. We have more brothers and sisters in the shelter who are in need of help.

Give, and it shall be given unto you; good measure, pressed down, and shaken together, and running over, shall men give into your bosom. For with the same measure that ye mete withal it shall be measured to you again. Luke 6:38

When you blessed the poor, the Lord Jesus will make sure your needs are met.

Luke quotes Jesus:
38Give, and it shall be given unto you; good measure, pressed down, and shaken together, and running over, shall men give into your bosom. For with the same measure that ye mete withal it shall be measured to you again.
"measure that ye mete withal it shall be measured to you again.
Luke 6:38

❊ *PRAYER POINTS* ❊

→ Spirit of laziness in my life and my family disappear now completely from today on, in Jesus name.

→ Lord Jesus, teach me how to bless the poor; all the ones you gave me in Jesus name.

→ Starting today, I will see no more generational poverty in my family, in Jesus name.

→ Father Lord, bless my family supernaturally in Jesus name.

Strategies for breaking the cycle of poverty

Chapter Three

1. Have a fearless attitude
2. Stop living a sinful life
3. Be born again
4. Stop Procrastination
5. Have a plan and goal
6. Write your plans and goals down

Have a fearless attitude

What is fear? Fear means an expectation of harm or pain, generally a painful emotion characterized by alarm, dread, disquiet.

→ Fear can keep you in poverty forever

→ Fear can make you to lose everything you own

→ Fear can keep you in a low state to keep you from attaining your goal in life.

→ Fear can make you bow down for your enemies

⁷For God hath not given us the spirit of fear; but of power, and of love, and of a sound mind. ²Timothy 1:7

To divorce poverty you must not allow the spirit of fear to dominate your life. The enemies want you to stay in fear and not enjoying the blessing of God upon your life.

Spirit of fear is terrible, dreadful, horrific, horrendous, abominable, and most sickening for Christians. To be honest with you I hate poverty! I cannot stand poverty and I abhor fear.

At one point in my life, I almost bend for my known enemies; but the spirit of God kept my head up. I held on and my Jesus delivered me from the hands of my enemies.

In the name of Jesus Christ of Nazareth, you will be delivered from the spirit of fear as you read this book.

The Devil uses the spirit of fear to destroy Christian lives so that they won't enjoy unlimited blessings from the Lord. Jesus died on the cross and took away our shame, poverty and sorrow completely. So, if you allow the spirit of fear to overtake you and rob God's blessings upon your life, I can assure you, you won't like it if you find out that the devil is only playing games with your intelligence.

But the good thing is it's *never* too late. You can still reclaim all that the enemy has rob you of at the mention of the name "JESUS."

Stop Living a Sinful Life

What is sin? It is anything contrary to Jehovah's personality, ways, standards, and will. Sin mars a person's relationship with God. Sin causes us to miss the mark. Even as an archer can shoot an arrow but miss his target, we can sin intentionally or by mistake.

According to the book of *Numbers 15:27-31,* sin is deeply ingrained in the human and creates a barrier between him and his Creator.

Now when one comes to Christ and learns of Him, the Bible says old things (manner, personalities and thinking) are passed away. Once you give your life to Christ Jesus of Nazareth, poverty is no more your portion. You are now King heirs and joint- heirs together with Christ.

12Wherefore, as by one man sin entered into the world, and death by sin; and so death passed upon all men, for that all have sinned: Romans 5:12

12Let not sin therefore reign in your mortal body, that ye should obey it in the lusts thereof. Romans 6:12

Many Christians are perpetual sinner. They come to Church dress holy, speak holy, ministering holy, but they are living a sinful lifestyle; thinking they are deceiving God. God sees everything that we do. Some spent their leisure time fornicating, clubbing, drinking, smoking, harassing church members, lies against anointed man and women of God expecting miracle to happen. **No one can deceive Jesus.**

God wants you to live in prosperity not in poverty, but a sinful lifestyle is disturbing and disrupting your breakthrough. Don't be a slave to sin.

Be Born Again

Pause and answer this question before moving on. Are you a born again Christian? The Bible says *that if any man be in Christ he is a new creature; old things are passed away and behold all things are become new. 2Corinthians 5:17*

Pray this prayer of repentance before you move on. Lord Jesus, remove the spirit of fear from me in Jesus name. I am a sinner. I come before you today. Wash me with your blood. Sanctify me and let me be clean. I believe that Jesus Christ is LORD, Amen.

Nicodemus saith unto him, How can a man be born when

he is old? can he enter the second time into his mother's womb, and be born? John 3:4

Whosoever is born of God doth not commit sin; for his seed remaineth in him: and he cannot sin, because he is born of God. 1 John 3:9

Once you give your life to Jesus, your life will encounter new beginnings. The Lord will always be there for you.

¹ Now the serpent was more subtil than any beast of the field which the LORD God had made. And he said unto the woman, Yea, hath God said, Ye shall not eat of every tree of the garden?

²And the woman said unto the serpent, We may eat of the fruit of the trees of the garden:

³But of the fruit of the tree which is in the midst of the garden, God hath said, Ye shall not eat of it, neither shall ye touch it, lest ye die.

⁴And the serpent said unto the woman, Ye shall not surely die:

⁵For God doth know that in the day ye eat thereof, then your eyes shall be opened, and ye shall be as gods, knowing good and evil.

⁶And when the woman saw that the tree was good for food, and that it was pleasant to the eyes, and a tree to be desired to make one wise, she took of the fruit thereof, and did eat, and gave also unto her husband with her; and he

did eat.
⁷And the eyes of them both were opened, and they knew
that they were naked; and they sewed fig leaves together,
and made themselves aprons. Genesis 3:1-7

When God created Adam and eve and put them in the Garden of Eden, they were blessed enough to resist Satan but they decided to go their way to eat the forbidden fruit of the knowledge of Good and Evil which is sinful to God and they faced the consequence of disobedience and separation from God.

You cannot choose the sin life and expect to get out of poverty.

Stop Procrastinations

Procrastinate means to put off intentionally and habitually; to put off intentionally the doing of something that should be done. For the procrastinator, putting things off has become a habit. As stress and pressure mount, he finds relief by pushing the task to the background and relishes his newly found "free time" until the pressure builds up again.

Always acknowledge that procrastination smothers all sense of motivation. The best way to abolish procrastination is to take a firm decision and make sure you complete it.

To everything there is a season, and a time to every purpose under the heaven: Ecclesiastes 3:1

The desire of the slothful killeth him; for his hands refuse to labour. Proverbs 22:25

You need to get up and tell God honestly that you're tired of fighting the clock and pray for wisdom in using time wisely.

The book of *Ecclesiastes 8:6* let us know that
6Because to every purpose there is time and judgment, therefore the misery of man is great upon him.

Change your way of keeping record. Get a paper or digital planner to track your tasks and appointments. You first have to be accountable to yourself, that's why recording your daily activities is so important.

17I said in mine heart, God shall judge the righteous and the wicked: for there is a time there for every purpose and for every work. Ecclesiastes 3:17 KJV

Have a Plans and goals

I have a good question for you; what is your goal in life?

And the Lord answered me: "Write the vision; make it plain on tablets, so he may run who reads it. For still the vision awaits its appointed time; it hastens to the end—it will not lie. If it seems slow, wait for it; it will surely come; it will not delay. Habakkuk 2:2-3

This is the word of God to Habakkuk. Make a habit of writing things down

Write the vision; make it plain on tablets, so he may run who reads it.

Your brain cannot assimilate everything. You need to start writing things such as visions, missions and strategies down. Make it a habit to always have pen and paper in your pocket.

The plans of the diligent lead surely to abundance, but everyone who is hasty comes only to poverty. Proverbs 21:5

Abundance is God plans for you and your family. Plan diligently and you will surely end up with good result.

13Brothers, I do not consider that I have made it my own. But one thing I do: forgetting what lies behind and straining forward to what lies ahead, 14I press on toward the goal for the prize of the upward call of God in Christ Jesus. Philippians 3:13-14

Apostle Paul makes it clear that we should not worry concerning things of the past. Things of the past will draw you backward. Remember to worry is to sin. Stop worrying; you are already a winner.

⊰ PRAYER POINTS ⊱

- → Spirit of fear and poverty departs from my life and enter no more in Jesus Name
- → Fear of the unknown in my life; disappear in the Mighty name of Jesus
- → Power and spirit sponsoring fear in my life be consumed by Holy Ghost fire
- → Lord Jesus, help me to break the spirit of poverty in my life in Jesus name

How to get out of Poverty

⌒∞∞∞⌒

Chapter Four

1. Be born again
2. Use God principles
3. Study the scripture
4. Realistic budget

Be Born Again

You must commit yourself, your finances, your family, and your life to Jesus Christ of Nazareth without looking back. Always remember what put you in poverty at first. Be absolutely honest about the faults and mistakes in your life, past or present, that may have caused your problem of debt. Keep this one thing fore-front in your mind.

What do ye imagine against the LORD? he will make an utter end: affliction shall not rise up the second time.
Nahum 1:9

Affliction cannot rise again. You must take the necessary steps to stop the affliction from rising again in your life through finances, health, and family.

Use God Principles

Many are still living their life with a nonchalant attitude. They are confused of whom they believe. Jesus is the only way. The Bible tells us in the book of *Hosea 4:6 – My people are destroyed for lack of knowledge* God's law is different from the world principle.

For his anger endureth but a moment; in his favour is life: weeping may endure for a night, but joy cometh in the morning. Psalm 30:5

God's principle may be tough; a little bite painful, but in following his principles, you will surely smile at last. His grace is what we need.

39Search the scriptures; for in them ye think ye have eternal life: and they are they which testify of me. John 5:39

Studying the scriptures will keep your ears and eyes open to the spirit of God's purpose in your life. God has a purpose for your life. You cannot keep on robbing yourself of God blessing. God created you in His own image. His plans for you are plans of Good not evil.

11For I know the thoughts that I think toward you, saith the LORD, thoughts of peace, and not of evil, to give you an expected end. Jeremiah 29:11

Realistic Budget

You need to ask yourself first, "Do I have a budget?"

Majority of people in our society don't have budgets, they go to the stores and buy what they did not budgeted for. Stores are set up to get most of your hard earned dollars. You must have accountability of how you spend your money or plan control. Think about this:

Bring ye all the tithes into the storehouse, that there may be meat in mine house, and prove me now herewith, saith the LORD of hosts, if I will not open you the windows of heaven, and pour you out a blessing, that there shall not be room enough to receive it. Malachi 3:10.

For your increase; payroll or otherwise follow this step:

→ Take out FIRST your tithes and offerings as number one spending before you take anything out else. Treat it as it were a BILL.

[10]Bring ye all the tithes into the storehouse, that there may be meat in mine house, and prove me now herewith, saith the LORD of hosts, if I will not open you the windows of

heaven, and pour you out a blessing, that there shall not be room enough to receive it. Malachi 3:10

22Without counsel purposes are disappointed: but in the multitude of counsellors they are established. Proverbs 15:22

Your budget will serve as a counsel to you. Once you have a list of what to buy and not to buy, you will be able to set some money apart for investment.

⟩⟨ SCRIPTURE POINTS ⟩⟨

- → Lord Jesus, counsel me over my finances, in Jesus name
- → Father Lord, help me to have a good budget, in Jesus name
- → Lord my God, teach me to be faithful in my tithes and offerings, in Jesus name.
- → Almighty God teaches me your word and let me understand, in Jesus Mighty name.

Be a Cheerful Giver

~~~oooOOooo~~~

Chapter Five

A cheerful giver will always have more than enough. Jesus Christ demonstrates the most cheerful giver on earth by giving himself to death for our sin.

⁷So let each one give as he purposes in his heart, not grudgingly or of necessity; for God loves a cheerful giver.
²Corinthians 9:7

Giving cheerfully will demonstrate Jesus Christ method of giving. Also Jesus demonstrates the love of giving by healing many in various occasions.

In the book of *Acts 20:35*, the word of the Lord Jesus says, *It is more blessed to give than to receive.* Your act of cheerful giving will reproduce in many folds. The same is true if you give sparingly, grudgingly or if you give nothing. The rewards for giving is more give. The penalty for not giving or giving with the wrong attitude is great loss.

Ye have sown much, and bring in little; ye eat, but ye have not enough; ye drink, but ye are not filled with drink; ye clothe you, but there is none warm; and he that earneth wages earneth wages to put it into a bag with holes. Haggai 1:6

Apostle Paul instructs us in his letter to Corinthians that whoever sow sparingly will also reap sparingly.

Whoever sows sparingly will also reap sparingly, and whoever sows generously will also reap generously 2 Corinthians 9:6

A cheerful giver will never lack anything. Make it a habit to support the mission of the church and evangelism. God is the rewarder of those that diligently seek him. God looked down on us and gave His only begetting Son to us.

For God so loved the world that He gave. John 3:16ᵃ

We would do well to remember that we are saved because our God so generously gave.

Looking at your expenses you may find it tough to give but you have to remember that it is the blessing of God that makes one rich without adding sorrow.

*The blessing of the LORD makes one rich,
And He adds no sorrow with it Proverbs 10:22*

⊰ PRAYER POINTS ⊱

→ Lord Jesus makes me rich (abundantly supplied) and adds no sorrow with my status, in Jesus name.

→ Almighty God, make me a cheerful giver in

Jesus name

→ Father Lord, teach me how to give. Thank you for letting me know that I don't give to get necessarily, but the law of sowing and reaping will run me down and take me over, in Jesus name.

→ Lord Jesus, makes me a blessing to others in Jesus name.

Poverty is a Sin

~~~

Chapter Six

Without shadow of doubt in our mind we should all understand that poverty is a sin. We need to use whatever means to fight and get rid of poverty in our cycle so that we can move to the next level of abundance. Because poverty is a sin you and poverty cannot reside in the same roof, body, spirit and soul.

For ye know the grace of our Lord Jesus Christ, that, though he was rich, yet for your sakes he became poor, that ye through his poverty might be rich. 2Corinthians 8:9

Some denominational circles believe getting rich is a sin. The Lord Jesus Christ came to make us rich. Let us define the word rich. Rich is to be abundantly supplied. Money and things are not the only thing that makes one rich. *3 John 1:2.* Poverty should not be what a Christian should experience in spirit soul or body. We are to lead a Godly life and at the same time, live in great abundant. I assume that poverty is the mark of religion *definitely* not the mark of Christianity. Rejecting poverty and move to the next level God gave His children open check in

> ¹⁴*If you ask anything in My name, I will do it.*
> *John 14:14*

The word "anything" is a powerful statement from God. If you ask for a lot of money He will give it to you. So why should you be poor if God gives you an open check to cash. God is our Father and His wealth is beyond human imagination or comprehension. We are heirs to His vast estate; He has given us a blank check, so it's up to us to fill everything we need in the blank spaces. God is our Father and His wealth is beyond human imagination or comprehension. We are heirs to His vast estate; He has given us a blank check, so it's up to us to fill everything we need in the blank spaces.

God's Grace is what we need to get out of poverty. According to 2 Timothy 2:1, this is how to take advantage of the grace in Christ Jesus. Don't let the world put the mark of religion on you; reject poverty because prosperity is your right and privilege in Christ.

> *The blessing of the LORD makes one rich,*
> *And He adds no sorrow with it*
> *Proverbs 10:22*

*The LORD the Shepherd of His People He makes me to
lie down in green pastures;
He leads me beside the still waters. Psalm 23:1-2*

When God makes you "to lie down in green
pastures; He leads me beside the still waters."
Means you will live in abundant blessing and not
in poverty.

You need to reject poverty and every power and
spirit that will takes you back to poverty again.
Poverty is not good.

Now that you understand what poverty is, think
about your present situation. Are you where you
want to be in life? If not stop procrastination,
Take a decision.

→ The Father took a decision and ran toward
his prodigal son in *Luke 15:20*

→ David took a decision and ran towards
Goliath in *1Samuel 17:48*

→ Paul took a decision and ran his race with
perseverance and endurance in *2Timothy
4:7*

→ Peter and John took a decision and ran to
the empty tomb of Jesus in *John 20:4*

You are a winner; you are conqueror, you are an
achiever, and you are unstoppable! Stop keeping
yourself in poverty, take a decision. Let your faith

propel you to your success.

God has given you power. Stronghold enemies cannot hold you back. Witches, warlocks and wizards cannot stop you. Take a decision today! You can fly above the level you are now in richness in Jesus mighty name.

❧ PRAYER POINTS ❧

→ Father in Heaven, I reject infirmity; I claim divine health, power, wealth, and greatness in the name of Jesus.

→ By the power of anointing, I reject curses, I claim God's blessing, in the name of Jesus.

→ Lord Jesus I reject poverty; I claim wealth and abundant prosperity, in the name of Jesus.

→ Almighty God I reject failure; I claim good success and prosperity, in the name of Jesus.

ABOUT THIS BOOK

The word of God in Luke 6:20-21 "Then he looked up at his disciples and said: 'Blessed are you who are poor, for yours is the kingdom of God. Blessed are you who are hungry now, for you will be filled. Blessed are you who weep now, for you will laugh."

At the point of your need, all you need to do is to pray to Jesus for supernatural release of abundance. Most believers don't realize they carry this power. Rather they beg for the thing they already have possession of; which is POWER and dominion.

This book will reveal the truth that you are destined as a believers to be blessed.
Your mouth carries the power of God. Use your mouth to proclaim your prosperity.

ABOUT THE AUTHOR

Bamidele Bello is the Presiding Pastor of Holy Mountain International Ministries (Blessed House) located on 7755 Belle Point Drive, Greenbelt, MD 20770, United States of America.

He is an anointed and gifted Teacher, Preacher, and Motivator. Bamidele Bello is known for his undiluted and life applicable teaching and preaching of God's Word.

Bamidele Bello is blessed in ministry with divine help and is married to his lovely wife Rhonda Bello with children.

Poverty I Divorce You Absolutely